W9-CXU-396

FIRST A GARDEN

FIRST A GARDEN

JON CARLOFTIS

PHOTOGRAPHS BY HELEN NORMAN

Published in 2005 by
Rockcastle River Trading Company
Route 5 Box 424
Livingston, Kentucky 40445
(606) 843-0854

Library of Congress Cataloging-in-Publication Data:
Carloftis, Jon
First A Garden by Jon Carloftis : photographs by Helen Norman
ISBN 0-9763496-0-4

Printed in Italy

First Edition

10 9 8 7 6 5 4 3 2 1

Riendeau Designs, Healdsburg, CA

Special thanks to Meredith Corporation for use of photography while shot on assignment for various publications
pages: 8, 10, 11, 30, 34, 36, 40, 43, 44, 56, 57, 58, 59, 62, 63, 112, 114, 115, 116, 117, 118, 199, 122, 123

Special thanks to my clients who have graciously provided us a glimpse into their private gardens:
Barbara Schwartz, Friederike and Jeremy Biggs, Jane and Michael Hoffman. Edward Norton, Jane Lauder,
Annie and Steve Murphy, Robert Hanley, Beverly and Bill Fortune, Melanie Acevedo and Richard White.

I WOULD LIKE TO DEDICATE THIS BOOK TO MOMMA AND DADDY

WHO RAISED US IN A WONDERFUL PLACE, IN THE COUNTRY OF EASTERN KENTUCKY.

THEY ENCOURAGED US TO FIND A CAREER THAT FOCUSED ON HAPPINESS

RATHER THAN MONEY. ALTHOUGH THEY TAUGHT US GOOD MANNERS AND

TO TREAT ALL PEOPLE EQUALLY, ONE OF THE MOST IMPORTANT LESSONS

WE LEARNED WAS TO BE PROUD OF OUR KENTUCKY HERITAGE.

THANK YOU SO MUCH FOR MAKING US FEEL WE COULD

ACCOMPLISH ANYTHING INTO WHICH WE PUT OUR HEART AND SOUL.

— JON

AS WE MOVE THROUGH OUR FAST-PACED LIVES, WE NEED TO REMEMBER TO LOOK TO THE

INNOCENCE OF OUR CHILDREN, AS IT REMINDS US TO SAVOR THE ESSENCE OF LIFE'S

EVERY MOMENT. I DEDICATE THIS BOOK TO PETER AND PATRICK FOR THEIR ABILITY

TO KEEP ME FRESH, AND IN TUNE WITH THE WONDER OF LIVING; AND TO MY HUSBAND

MARK, FOR HIS CONSTANT ENCOURAGEMENT, LOVE AND SUPPORT. I CHERISH YOU ALL.

— HELEN

CONTENTS

WE HAVE BEEN TAUGHT THAT LIFE BEGINS IN THE GARDEN.

This is, after all, where life's promise of tomorrow is kept.

When my youngest brother, Jon, left our Kentucky home on the Rockcastle River and moved to New York City, we couldn't understand why. A few years later he showed us photographs of a small 1850's farmhouse just across a covered bridge in Bucks County, Pennsylvania. After my first visit it struck me that this brother had completely lost his mind. Although it did have running water, the house was barely inhabitable. And while I slept on old plank floors in the front room, my brother was busy planting a garden, a garden that made the house beside the road a home.

Your home awaits a garden. Whether a Baronial estate, an apartment above the city streets, or a modest cottage beside the road, it is the garden that really defines the home.

From container gardens on rooftops, to colorful borders and allees, a garden's outdoor "rooms" expand the home's living space and connect the resident with a wonderful nature to explore.

Every home deserves a garden, and the beautiful gardens designed by Jon Carloftis captured on these pages through the lens of Helen Norman, provide the residents with great rewards and a lifetime of pleasure every time they open the garden gate.

– Buzz Carloftis

MY OLD KENTUCKY HOME

STILL AN INSPIRATION

I was raised near Livingston on a remote stretch of land bordering lower Kentucky's Rockcastle River. By today's standards, my upbringing might be considered rather simple. My family's closest neighbors lived two miles downriver and four miles upriver. We had neither a telephone until 1969 nor a TV until 1985, and even now my family rarely turns the TV on.

In 1955, Momma and Daddy started their business, a tourist shop for people traveling the Dixie Highway. During this "age of innocence", I believe children knew better how to entertain themselves by exploring their natural surroundings. My family's land was surrounded by the Daniel Boone National Forest. My father and I took long walks along the Rockcastle River weekly to check our home's water supply from a spring on our property two miles away. By the time I was a teenager, I knew most of the names of the native trees, shrubs and flowers that grew along the path.

I try to return to Livingston at least once a month. With special help from my sister Betsy and brother Buzz, Momma still runs Rockcastle River Trading Company, our beautiful home and garden store. A footbridge connects the store to our two-story, English red Colonial home. The air is fragrant with gardenias, phlox and mint. A healthy butterfly bush nearly hides the front door entrance.

Daddy transplanted some things from the woods while he was alive. I have taken over from there by adding additional landscape and architectural structures including an arbor, red cedar pergola, carriage house, and potting shed. I further added a bubbling stone fountain, rose and vegetable gardens and koi pond to compliment Daddy's work. I would like to think that I've added a surprise around every corner. A restored blacksmith's shop and a rustic one-room schoolhouse used as a guest house are also enjoyed by everyone who visits.

Rest and relaxation at times is what I hope for when I return to Livingston. But in reality, I hit the ground running each day with garden design projects, replenishing and redesigning the store, speaking engagements and of course family gatherings. I simply cannot wait to get my hands on the land itself, taking care of the gardens once again. I feel responsible for keeping everything as lush and as beautiful as it should be.

Home is where my horticulture career began. This family-owned land has a personality, a soul – history. It inspired me as a child. It jump-starts me now and always will. Whenever I stroll along the Rockcastle River, I feel content, humbled and blessed.

The Crossing *– Every time we leave our home, we embark upon a journey...*

Colonial Vegetable Garden *– Living off the land – with style*

The Old Guard – Bertha and Daisy watch over the vegetable garden

The Potting Shed – *A gardener's room with a view*

THE BIG APPLE

EARLY ADVENTURES
I arrived in New York City in June of 1988, fresh out of college – green as grass. My original plan was to stay the summer with a friend, earn a meager living hauling dirt, enjoy the city in my spare time, then move back to Kentucky in the fall to start my own business as a landscape designer. My plans would change.

I discovered I loved the physical labor of gardening, a task more challenging at the core of the Big Apple – New York City. I grew increasingly fascinated with using my hands to create beauty in unexpected places. Early clients and friends admired my dedication and hard work and tempted me with ideas of more rewarding work along with the promise of spring. I printed business cards which read: "Jon Carloftis, Rooftop Garden Designer", perhaps a bit creative given I had never set foot on a rooftop before. I handed my cards to doormen, bellhops and elevator men throughout the Upper East Side. A phone call from a couple living in a Park Avenue penthouse with a wraparound terrace would spark my career in New York City.

Dining Out – *"I'd like the table with the best view..."*

When first visiting their apartment, I would gaze open-mouthed at their vast collection of magnificent modern art. How could I make this magnificent home more beautiful? She would say to me: "I want you to feel this art– and then take it outdoors". You might imagine my first thoughts. I would soon learn what she meant. The same edginess and aggressive sophistication which was her calling card indoors, needed to continue outside. No dainty tulips for this woman. No sweet petunias or simple boxwood. Cute little hyacinth would not feed her soul. She was more a contorted filbert. I had to create something totally unexpected-- just for her.

"Long before customization comes watching, listening and learning" – this would be one of the best lessons I would ever learn. The likelihood of other lessons learned in this different place would keep me in New York City.

I'm considered by most people to be lucky. But luck has nothing to do with one's actions and hard work. A girlfriend of mine reminds me of this. "Luck is when you buy a lottery ticket and win," she says. I've taken a thousand tiny steps to build the career I enjoy today – landscape designer, lecturer, writer, storeowner. The most painful but rewarding steps I have taken are invisible to most.

Artful Seating – 60's metal furniture surrounded by flora and fauna

Sitting on Top of the World – *A quiet retreat from the hustle and bustle*

ANNUALS

You may consider planting annuals every year (hence the name). They'll bloom all season long. A few are self-seeding which can be either a blessing or a bane. All of these selections are silver and white, the mainstays of my color choices. They "light up" any garden, especially effective when you're entertaining at night.

Cosmos bipinnatus (cosmos)
Needs full sun.
Wispy, fernlike foliage with happy, daisy-like flowers that measure two to three inches. By late summer, they'll begin to wane, but cooler fall temperatures revive them before the frost finally takes them away.

Sutera (bacopa)
Needs full sun.
The best of the "creepers." Its hard to imagine container gardens before this wonderful variety became readily available. Within a single season, it will spill over the edges of your container with multitudes of flowers. The foliage has a pleasant scent when brushed.

Helichrysum petiolare (licorice vine)
Needs full sun to partial shade.
An extremely fast grower which can take over other plantings. I'd prefer to prune something than beg it to grow, especially as handsome as this plant is.

Left: Cleome spinosa (spider flower)

Needs full sun.

By midsummer, these spiky, spidery flowers are four to five feet tall and work well as a backdrop for flower beds. The good news: they reseed with a vengeance and come back in the most unexpected places. Some people consider that a nuisance, but I love it.

Right: Senecio cineraria 'cirrus' (dusty miller)

Needs full sun.

The old variety is fine, but this newer variety is absolutely luxurious, with thick, velvety leaves. It's a great example of living better through technology. Cut big bunches and bring them indoors for all of your vases.

Below: Impatiens walleriana (impatience)

Needs partial shade to shade.

Ideal for shadier areas to lighten things up. This annual is so simple, so easy and elegant. Anyone who doesn't like this plant arouses my suspicions!

Calibrachoa x hybriduus (mission bells)

Needs full sun to partial shade.

Looks similar to a petunia without the need for deadheading. After making the leap, I've never looked back. If only someone could add the petunia's delightful spicy scent, this annual might move closer to the top of my list.

Nicotiana alata (flowering tobacco)

Needs sun to partial shade.

The short varieties are fine. But if you have the space, the old-fashioned tall variety is spectacular given its flowers and fragrance which becomes heavier at night.

FIRST, A GARDEN...

When I bought my 1850's Pennsylvania farmhouse in 1990, I couldn't wait to get started on the garden. Before any home improvement, I created first an allee of trees leading visitors from the garage to the house. Southerners love any journey through a majestic, tree-lined path.

For my allee, I used fast-growing, inexpensive, Bradford pear trees. Over the next few years, these trees would grow tall and together to create a tunnel. Today, 15 years later, they are magnificent – a show stopper. In the spring, they're literally white with blooms. In the summer, they're rich forest green. In the fall, they turn a beet-red and dark burgundy. I keep them clipped in a box shape and up-light them with a soft-glowing, hidden lamp.

To me, even the most simple plants can be combined or used to create an incredible result.

A Centerpiece – *The focal point of my back garden*

Hot Summer Afternoon – *But fall will soon be here*

Taking the Ordinary to the Extraordinary – *Common Bradford pear trees create a majestic allee*

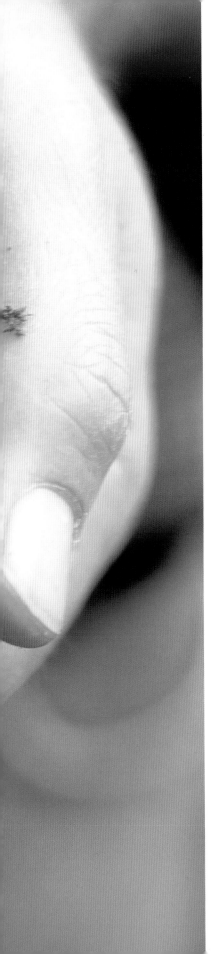

THE DIRT CONNECTION

When I was in second grade, I was assigned a simple but amazing project. As instructed, I laid stones in a pickle jar, covered them with dirt, sprinkled in grass seed, and added water. In the covered jar green grass would soon grow from these ugly, brown pellets. Let nature take its course – something dried up and dull can metamorphose into something lush and gorgeous.

On the first warm day of every year, even if it arrives in early February, we get this urge to dig in the dirt. It's a primal connection. March and April are ideal for planting. After the ground's retained water has frozen, expanded, and thawed once again, the soil is ready for easier tilling. It's like rich, brown butter.

There is nothing like delving deep into velvety smooth soil and knowing that, if you care for the soil properly, the plant will grow strong and healthy. It's a reciprocal friendship.

Bucks County Potting Shed – *The space under the screened porch makes a fine storage area for tools*

A Spring Experiment – *Fresh cuttings will soon root*

A Jump-start on Spring – *Start seedlings indoors for spring plantings*

Under Glass – *Bell jars & seedlings make an unusual centerpiece*

TOOLS

There are as many garden gadgets out there as kitchen gadgets. The best cooks I know use only a few knives and good cookware to make the best meals. When it all comes down to it, these are the tools that I really use, almost everyday. A good leaf rake would be number nine...

Felco Brand Pruners

Borrow my shovel, borrow my wheelbarrow, but don't touch my Felco pruners. I don't even feel completely dressed without a pair in my back pocket. As with most high quality tools, they cost a bit more, but will last for years. And, the blade can be replaced unlike other inferior ones.

Spade

I have broken my share of shovels in my gardening career. It took several years before finding this aluminum and plastic handled spade that slices through soil and root systems equally as well. Feel the weight and make sure it is comfortable before you buy.

Folding Pruning Saw

For larger branches, I prefer this tool with its ferocious "teeth" rather than get out my problematic chain saw. Tree pruning saws cut on the way back of the motion rather than forward like a regular wood saw. It is amazing what a difference this makes when you are 12' up in a tree, pruning away.

Left: Shears

A sharp pair brings out the Edward Scissorhands in all of us. Perfect for creating "clouds" in my American boxwood and for making sharp edges in my English boxwood. Warning: too much testosterone and a sharp pair do not mix.

Right: Trowel

I use a trowel practically everyday from March through December. Buy only solid construction made out of metal alloy instead of a handle and scoop connected by a rivet. It will last much longer in less than perfect soil.

Below: Dibble

In the spring, after the soil has been worked into a rich consistency of butter, this tool is useful in the vegetable garden for onions and planting seedlings. Attach a string to two of them to create a straight line.

Weeder

Perhaps the most important tool of all in the heat of summer when weeds grow like, well, a weed. For dandelions, it can get the root without disturbing too much around it.

Lopper

For quick pruning on medium size branches, the lopper makes fast work for forsythia, lilacs and wisteria. I prefer by-pass rather than anvil types; it makes a cleaner cut.

WHY WE LOVE FLOWERS

Flowers have a universal appeal. No one can walk away unmoved. They appeal to so many of our senses. We relish the sight of them, the feel of them, their glorious fragrance.

Flowers are symbolic, with roses connoting strong emotions, violets sweetness, orchids sophistication and daisies youthful innocence. Send someone a bouquet and you'll convey a very special message.

Regardless of how complex and technical our lives become, we will always be mesmerized by one of nature's loveliest and most abundant gifts.

Beauty and a Feast – *Dining al fresco*

Early to Rise – *Breakfast under the grape arbor*

COLORFUL ANNUALS

How can you not like a plant that blooms from the last frost in the spring until the first frost in the fall? These annuals keep on going with little work other than the occasional pruning, deadheading, and fertilizing. Give these winners a try!

Topaeolum majus (nasturtium)
Needs full sun to partial shade.
I first began planting these flowers as easy, no-fuss projects for my clients' children. They soon became a favorite in all of my herb gardens and window boxes. Now that the color orange has become a big part of my life (we are constantly changing, thank goodness), nasturtiums are in every garden I create.

Verbena hybrida (verbena)
Needs full sun.
Its fine leaves will creep over your garden's edges and bloom continuously all summer long. It is available in other colors, but purple is my favorite.

Dahlia (dahlia)
Needs full sun.
This good old Southern plant reminds me of being a child and standing shorter than it was! Flowers can be huge or else a profusion of small blooms-- a show stopper either way. Many colors are available.

Left: Catharanthus rosea (vinca)
Needs full sun.
I first started using this plant when my client with arthritis asked me for flowers that she did not have to deadhead. When I found out how easy and rewarding vinca was, it became a must have in every garden.

Right: Tagetes patula (French marigold)
Needs full sun.
One of those common flowers that people love to hate, because they tend to surround gas pumps and shopping malls-- but if you stand back and accept them for what they are, you will fall in love. Not only do marigolds readily accept tough conditions, they repel many harmful insects.

Below: Coleus x hybridus (garden coleus)
Need full sun to partial shade.
Every color and shape imaginable, with many new (and forgotten old) varieties. The leaves make a bold statement and mix well with flowers of any color. In late summer and early fall they are in their glory.

Salvia farinacea 'Victoria' (mealy blue sage)
Needs full sun.
Rich, green foliage with spectacular spikes of purple blossoms (the white version is not as vigorous) which lasts well into fall.

Plumbago auriculata (plumbago)
Needs full sun.
The hotter it gets, the better plumbago blooms, even in small containers. Not many plants produce this true blue color (it also comes in white) but it is spectacular in August and September. The arching branches add an interesting form.

Petite Jardin *– A barnyard is transformed into a lush retreat*

Reach for the Sky – Delphiniums and foxglove tower above the garden

PERENNIALS

EIGHT BEST   In general, perennials come back each year with hearty blooms for a few weeks, at some point in the season. A perennial can last for decades (peonies up to 75 years). I choose them mainly for the foliage. The blooms are just an added bonus.

Sedum herbstfreude 'autumn joy' (autumn joy sedum)
Needs full sun.
Another drought-tolerant perennial that's one of the easiest plants to grow. For most of the season its color is that wonderful chartreuse that I love. The actual blooms are a sort of mauve/pink that isn't so great– but by fall the combination seems to work.

Miscanthus sinensis (maidenhair grass)
Needs full sun.
Grasses are tough, drought-tolerant, disease and insect-resistent-- even deer-proof! I like to leave the wheat-colored foliage alone all winter before cutting it back in the spring. There are many varieties available, but I keep returning to this one.

Echinacea purpurea (purple coneflower)
Needs full sun to partial shade.
The intriguing and gorgeous color combination of purple, pink, orange and yellow is an odd one but always works for me. Flowers bloom in midsummer and attract butterflies by the hundreds.

Left: Phlox paniculata (garden phlox)
Needs sun to partial shade.
Old-fashioned, tall, sweet-smelling and reliable. No garden is complete without it. They grew wild along the banks of the Rockcastle River, filling the air with sweet perfume.

Right: Hemerocallis (day lily)
Needs full sun.
Its sword-shaped leaves are essential, I think, in any garden. The bonus: up to three months of blooms in an ever-expanding array of colors. Recently, many fragrant varieties are being introduced.

Below: Hosta
Needs partial to full shade.
Ideal for filling your garden's shadier areas. There's a variety for everyone but 'Sieboldiana' and 'Sum and Substance' are my personal favorites.

Iris varieties
Needs full sun.
Whether you choose old-fashioned German, the 'Wild Flag' or the Siberian, the foliage is amazing-- a must-have in every garden I've ever designed.

Rudbeckia hirta (black-eyed Susan)
Needs full sun.
When I tried to decide what to plant in the tiny two-foot space between my fence and the road, I knew these would fit the bill. Despite scorching heat in July and trucks spraying salt in December, these flowers somehow keep on blooming every summer and into fall.

IN YOUR "ROOMS"

When transforming a huge expanse of grass and trees or an empty terrace
into something more beautiful, most people don't know where to begin.
The answer is surprisingly simple. Visually divide the space into "rooms"
using plants and architectural elements. Remember, there's nothing cozy or
intimate about a football field.

Finish one section at a time, then move on. It takes longer, but it's also easier
to manage. You'll feel a sense of accomplishment much sooner. A series of
small mountains become one large one before you know it.

Helen's Outdoor Room *– An intimate dining area in the middle of 130 acres*

Swing Time – *The meeting of town and country*

The Sitting Room – *A place to retire after dinner*

T R E E S

Trees form a natural structure for your garden, regardless whether they are situated on a balcony or they cover an entire estate. I prefer trees with year-round interest. In fact, winter is when I enjoy them most. During the remaining three seasons, leaves and flowers may snare your attention; but with winter's bareness, a tree's true shape stands out.

Comus florida (dogwood)
Needs sun to partial shade.
The native variety, Comus florida, is a sight to behold in the spring. The Asian version, Comus kousa, blooms a month later with similar flowering, great leaves and huge red fruits in maturity. Blooming views are better from above, on an elevated deck or from a second-story window.

Tsuga canadensis (hemlock)
Needs partial shade.
This is certainly the most elegant of the evergreens, with its graceful branches especially when covered with snow. If you spot one growing wild in the woods, the feeling is magical. Just remember the moist soil conditions it requires.

Quercus phellos (willow oak)
Needs full sun.
Every oak is beautiful to me. This option, with its slender bright green leaves in the spring, and a dark, glossy green in summer, allows light to filter underneath for additional plantings. The narrow leaves give a much finer texture.

Left: Cercis canadensis (Eastern redbud)
Needs sun to partial shade.
When illegal strip mining for coal took place in Kentucky, this tree was the first to spring up amidst such harsh conditions. That toughness, along with reddish-pink blooms in the spring, heart-shaped leaves in the summer and handsome grey bark in the winter, all make it a no-fail choice.

Right: Magnolia soulangiana (saucer magnolia)
Needs full sun to partial shade.
Actually, any magnolia works for me. Check out the Magnolia soulangiana (saucer magnolia) and the Magnolia stellata (star magnolia) at the Frick Museum in New York City--there are no better specimens. But the Southern variety (Magnolia grandifolia) has lustrous leaves all year, with large, white lemon scented blossoms. It is well worth the leaf litter.

Below: Cryptomeria japonica (Japanese cedar)
Needs full sun to partial shade.
With its fine-textured needles and wonderful shape, this is one of my crowd-pleasers. I planted twelve along the fence at my home in Kentucky, and everyone now claims it as a favorite.

Pinus umbraculifera (umbrella pine)
Needs full sun.
Pines are amazingly tough trees that can offer many landscape solutions. This is one everyone will ask about when they visit your garden--so soft, so unusual, so incredible-looking. This is a guaranteed showstopper.

Acer palmatum (Japanese maple)
Needs full sun to partial shade.
They're the first "special" trees that many people plant. Every variety is wonderful to me, especially the coral bark, because of its brilliant colored branches in the winter.

IF YOU LISTEN,

IT WILL SPEAK

When I was growing up, Mrs. Gabbard, my family's closest neighbor, treated us with the most amazing garden. Having been an army wife, this gardening wizard lived all over the world, collecting seeds along the way. Again and again, I heard her say, "Nature will tell you what you can and cannot do." Again and again, I learned how right she was. Unfortunately, sometimes I would learn the hard way.

For years I tried to grow roses along one side of my garage. And year after year I ripped them out when they started looking like those you had pressed between the pages of a scrapbook. I relented ultimately turning to ornamental grasses, cleome and dahlias.

I bought rhododendrons the first year I moved to Bucks County. I wanted the back garden to look like home in Kentucky, where the cultivated part fades seamlessly into the wilderness. However juglone, a substance produced by black walnut trees on my property, would prove lethal to my rhododendrons. It's survival of the fittest even in the plant world. Take notes.

There are loopholes, too. My heirloom tomatoes are grown in old whiskey barrels while redbuds, andromedas, and native ferns co-exist peacefully with the black walnuts.

Mrs. Gabbard is almost 100 years and still gardens a bit. She is always looking for a new seed or plant to put in her garden with hopes of a happy return.

Mrs. Gabbard taught me a lifetime in just a few words.

A Nice Reflection on You – *Mirrored lattice creates the illusion of a larger space*

Make a Wish – *An Italian ceramic fountain adorns a wall of ivy*

Everyone has a view they want to see...

And one they want to camouflage

Sweet Dreams – *Relaxing atop the big city*

SHRUBS

Shrubs underscore trees and provide a visual stairstep downward from the vertical effects of forests and buildings. When people think of old-fashioned plants, they often recall shrubs from childhood. Because of their year-round permanence, as opposed to perennials which die down in the winter, and because they are generally at eye-level, it's important to consider their appearance throughout all four seasons. Notice that most of my favorites are evergreens!

Juniperus chinensis 'robusta green' (robusta green juniper)
Needs full sun.
Always my favorite upright juniper because it's fairly straight-growing, like an exclamation point, without being too perfect like the dwarf Alberta spruce, or too wild like the Hollywood juniper. Wind, drought, heat and cold-tolerance, along with beautiful gray berries, make this shrub even more attractive.

Pieris japonica (Japanese andromeda)
Needs full sun to partial shade.
Shade-tolerant and deer-resistant, it blooms in early spring with a white panicle and is much hardier than a rhododendron or azalea.

Buxus sempervirens (American boxwood)
Needs full sun to partial shade.
I can't even imagine a garden without boxwood. Let it grow naturally, or lightly clip it into cloud formations. Tolerant of most conditions other than winter wind or "wet feet."

Left: Hydrangea 'tardiva' (southern hydrangea)
Needs partial shade.
I've never met a hydrangea I didn't like. They are all good, but
this one springs to life in late summer, when we can all use a jolt
of excitement.

Right: Chamaecyparis obtusa 'nana' (dwarf hinoki cypress)
Needs full sun.
An evergreen with needles that have a swirl effect. If a plant has
a personality, this is Mr. or Miss Congeniality. Even small ones will
seem to take on human or animal shape.

Below: Chamaecyparis pisifera 'boulevard' (boulevard cypress)
Needs full sun.
Here's that grayish-blue color that I love in the form of an evergreen
shrub. Its soft needles make it pleasant to touch, and the color works
well with dark greens.

Euonymus alata 'compacta' (burning bush)
Needs full sun to partial shade.
Whether it's spring's new, bright green leaves,
summer's rich, dark ones, autumn's bright red
leaves or winter's beautiful winged stems, this is
a most beautiful shrub. Tough beyond belief, it
tolerates almost any conditions.

Vitex agnus-castus (chaste tree)
Needs full sun to shade.
Another late-bloomer that tolerates wet soil. It likes water
so much, in fact, that I'll place it at the edge of a pond along
with flag iris and willows. The look is similar to a butterfly
bush, but it's cleaner, not quite so wild in growth.

THE INTERIOR-EXTERIOR CONNECTION

Want to know which hues to choose for your garden? Take a look inside – in your living room, dining room, kitchen, or perhaps your bedroom. Having trouble deciding whether to go Zen-like minimal or full-blown eye-catching? Study your own color choices in art and accessories.

Occasionally it's fun to stage a complete departure, with a super-simple interior filled with neutrals, and then stepping outside into a kaleidoscope of hot oranges, moon yellows and acid greens. But most people like the consistency of complementary shades rather than too many eye-poppers.

If you aren't sure how to make your garden look like an extension of your home, the answer is probably staring you right in the face.

My Kind of Camping – *A bedroom outdoors with all the comforts of home*

The Screening Room – *Beautiful pictures of nature*

Glass Houses *– A conservatory can be much more than a growing space*

EVEN WINTER
CAN BE LOVELY

When the killing frosts have taken all but the memories of the flora and fauna of the summer, I have already brought in my favorite tropical plants to over-winter. Instead of hiding them in the basement with a grow light, I like to place them all over the house to remind me that no matter how harsh the winter may be, spring is always around the corner. If the garden didn't turn out as well as planned, we always have next year to try again.

Fresh – Cool greens make for a soothing dining experience

Afternoon Delight – *A sleigh bed is the perfect day bed*

Spring Showers – *Most tropical plants love this steamy environment*

Mini Greenhouse – My bathroom is a tropical paradise in the winter

WHAT REALLY MAKES

A GARDEN BEAUTIFUL

Trying to define a beautiful garden is like trying to describe a beautiful woman. Each one is unique and lovely in its own way.

But make no mistake, there are key elements characteristic of every great garden – a comfortable place to sit, the sound of water, a view of certain areas while keeping some parts of the garden a mystery, and most of all, restraint. Other than that, a beautiful garden just needs to be healthy, and it needs to be loved.

Once it begins to bloom, you'll realize that it's giving you something quite marvelous in return for all the time and energy you've spent. It's showing you something new and different every time you see it. It's allowing you to witness the incredible intelligence, synchronicity and wisdom of nature.

But the more important lesson is that a garden is never really finished. No matter how beautiful it looks right now, it will forever be a work in progress.

Tea Time – *Grape vines provide shade from the afternoon sun*

A Splash of Color – Water gardening's visual rewards

Sitting Pretty – *Enjoy the fruits of your labor*

Welcome! – *Make the first impression a good one*

VINES

EIGHT BEST   A simple vine can visually connect man-made structures to the earth. Especially for new houses without surrounding trees, a vine can give age in just one season. Here are the best eight.

Ipomoea batatas (sweet potato vine)
Needs full sun.
Although this annual vine is used primarily as a "creeper" over the edge of containers, it will climb if there is something to wrap around. The color is that magnificent acid green that works so well with most other colors and at the end of the season, big edible sweet potatoes are left underneath the soil. You will have to cut it back occasionally, but I would rather beat something back than beg it to grow.

Hedera helix (English ivy)
Needs full sun to shade.
An old saying goes, "the first year it sleeps, the second year it creeps and the third year it leaps." Well, this pretty much says it all. And it is evergreen which makes it useful for winter gardens.

Clematis paniculata (sweet autumn clematis)
Needs full sun to partial shade.
Of all the clematis varieties, this is the one I love. It is not finicky, has few pests, blooms when most plants are finished and seeds like mad. I've planted them in every garden I've ever created.

Left: Wisteria sinensis (wisteria)
Needs full sun to shade.

Tough, super-fast grower, strangling... these are just a few adjectives to describe wisteria. It scares many people, but no other vine quite covers an arbor like wisteria. The old question is how to get them to bloom. First, buy a plant at the nursery that is in bloom to insure it is a bloomer and then don't give it fertilizer because this will only encourage green growth. Then, they bloom when they are damn ready. The best bloomers I've seen grow out of a crack in a sidewalk in New York City.

Right: Ipomoea (morning glory)
Needs full sun.

Soak the seeds in water for a day or so until the hard seed coat opens. Start them indoors or directly into the soil and soon you will have heart-shaped leaves with a bright pastel flower that open with a cheerfulness every morning. This is a "happy" flower for me.

Below: Campsis radicans (trumpet vine)
Needs full sun to partial shade.

This is another native vine that covers the walking bridge at my family home in Kentucky and the whole back of my farmhouse in Pennsylvania. With age, the vine gets a twisted trunk which is striking in the winter and its bloom season lasts from mid-summer to late fall. If you plant it, the hummingbirds will come visit. The yellow version is called 'Flava'.

Madevillea sanderi (mandevillea)
Needs full sun to partial shade.

As with most tropicals, this vine will bloom and bloom with very little root space and extremely hot temperatures – in other words, ideal for that cool little antique urn that is too small for anything to grow. This is the perfect vine for profuse flowers. They are also easy to over-winter for the next year.

Parthenocissus quinquefolia (Virginia creeper)
Needs full sun to shade.

This vine grows wild in both of my gardens in Kentucky and Pennsylvania. Although it looks similar to poison ivy ("leaves three, let it be...") this five leafed vine is a vigorous grower in the shade or the sun, city or country. Brilliant red foliage in the fall makes a display like non other and the bare vines are handsome on winter walls.

NATURE IS BRILLIANT IN ITS MANY PARADOXES.

THE MOST BEAUTIFUL SOULS CAN SHOW UP

IN THE HUMBLEST OF PACKAGES.

AND THE LOVELIEST GARDENS ARE OFTEN THOSE

WHERE NOBODY APPEARS TO HAVE FUSSED VERY MUCH.